AUSSIE SLANG DOWN UNDER

Pictorial Press Australia

This edition published by Pictorial Press Australia
PO Box 388 Corinda Brisbane Qld 4075 Australia
Ph 07 3716 01 04 Fax 07 3716 01 05
robert@pictorialpress.com.au

Reprinted 2012
Reprinted 2013
Reprinted 2014
Reprinted 2016

ISBN 978 1 876561 09 3

Compiling by Robert Brown, Sue Tester, Selena Webber

Produced by Jade Productions

AUSSIE SLANG DOWN UNDER

Australian slang utilises humour, wit, rhymes, bizarre experiences from the bush to the beach, familiar and personal to portray how experiences shape language and identity. For example, *'have a burl'* at something is similar to *'have a crack'*, and both phrases reflect a history of Australian improvisation and hard work as part of working in the bush.

Please note that some of the words and expressions in **Aussie Slang Down Under** may cause offence. It is not recommended to use such words and expressions, but they have been included as **Aussie Slang Down Under** is a book about the use of language whether it be good or bad.

A1   first class
ABC   Australian Broadcasting Corporation or Aunty
AC DC   bisexual
AFL   Australian football league
AO   adults only
APC   hand-wash arm pits and crotch
A big deal   important, serious
A bit much   rude, excessive
A bit rich   over-priced
A okay   very good
A over t/Arse over tit   falling over, stumbling
A real shit   a horrible person
Above board   legal
Abso-bloody-lutely   positively yes
Ace   the best, very good
Act the goat   foolish behaviour
Adams ale   water
Aerial ping pong   Australian Rules Football
Aggro   aggressive behaviour
Aggy pipe   terracotta drainage pipe
Akubra   a wide-brimmed hat
Al Capone   telephone
Alice, the   Alice Springs
Alko   an alcoholic, heavy drinker
All ears   listening attentively
All piss and wind   insincere, boastful
All rounder   good at many tasks or sports
All smiles   happy
All systems go   ready
Alrighty   okay, yes

Akubra is a popular brand of **Aussie** fur felt hats. The wide brim is a typical part of **Ozzie** culture.

Always in the shit   always in trouble
Always on the go   always busy
Amber fluid   beer
Ambo   ambulance
Ammo   ammunition
Amp   1. amplifier; 2. get excited
Anal   1. fussy, perfectionist, neat; 2. obsessive
Ankle biter   infant or young child
ANZAC   Australian and New Zealand Army Corps
Anchors   car brakes
Ant's pants   very good
Ape shit   raving mad
Apple Isle   Tasmania
Apples, she'll be   it'll be all right
Argue the toss   disagree
Argy bargy   an argument
Around the bend   crazy, mad
Arse end   worst part, tail end
Arse into gear   get going, moving, start
Arse off   depart
Arsey   very lucky
Arthur or Martha   a state of confusion
Arvo   afternoon
As crook as a dog   very unwell
As if   expression of complete disagreement, disbelief
As pissed as a newt   very drunk
As rough as guts   1. poor workmanship, rough; 2. uncouth person
As the crow flies   travel in a direct line
At death's door   dying, seriously ill
At full tilt   at full speed

ANZAC Day, 25th April is an important national occasion. It marks the anniversary of the first major military action fought by Australian and New Zealand forces in the Battle of Gallipoli during the First World War. The soldiers became known as **ANZACs**.

At odds   disagreement
At the crack of dawn   daybreak
At the drop of a hat   immediately
At the wheel   in control, in charge
Atta boy   approval
Aussie/Ozzie   an Australian person
Aussie battler   a working class person
Aussie rules   Australian football
Aussie salute   brushing away flies with your hand
'Ave a go   do something, get started
Avos   avocados
Awesome   1. excellent; 2. high quality
Axe/Axed   dismissed, get the sack
BBQ   barbeque
BYO   1. bring your own alcohol; 2. unlicensed restaurant
Back down   retreat from an argument
Back of beyond   a remote area
Back of Bourke   remote outback area
Backhander   hit with the back of the hand
Bad mouth   criticise unfavourably
Bad trot   period of misfortunes and bad luck
Bag   1. claim first; 2. unattractive woman
Bag of fruit   a suit
Bail out   to depart, leave a situation
Bail up   to physically corner somebody
Ball and chain   wife
Balmain bug   crab or crustacean
Banana bender   a Queenslander
Banged up   pregnant
Banjo   1. frying pan; 2. a shovel

Barbie barbeque
Banker a river or stream in flood
Barney an argument or fight
Barra fish called a Barramundi
Barrack to cheer on a sporting team
Bash 1. attempt; 2. party; 3. assault someone
Batch living on one's own
Bathers swimming costume
Battler one who struggles in life
Beanie knitted brimless cap
Beaut/beauty fantastic, excellent
Bee's knees great, fantastic
Beer belly beer drinking paunch
Belly-ache to complain
Belly-button navel
Bellyful too much of anything
Belt 1. move quickly; 2. hit
Bender drinking binge
Bend the elbow a heavy drinker
Betcha I bet you
Better half wife
Bevan lout, hooligan
Bewdie 1. beautiful, good; 2. approval
Bible basher a religious person
Biddie old woman
Bikkie biscuit
Big girl's blouse 1. effeminate male; 2. timid
Big red male red kangaroo
Big smoke a big city, usually a capital city
Big spit vomit

Rock on over for a **barbie** Saturday **arvo**. There'll be **heaps** of **snags**, **prawns** and **chook**. **BYO**, down a few **coldies** and **veg out**.

Big-note oneself   to boast or brag about oneself

Billabong   a waterhole

Billycan (billy)   a metal container to brew tea over the campfire

Billycart   homemade cart steered by ropes

Bin   garbage can

Bindi   plant with prickly seeds

Bingle   a minor car crash

Birthday suit   naked

Bite ya bum   be quiet, shut up

Bitser   an animal or person of mixed blood

Bizzo   doing business

Black stump, beyond the   long distance away

Blind   very drunk person

Blind Freddie   an unperceptive person

Blob   1. a fat person; 2. cricket score; out with no runs

Blockie   drive around the block

Bloke   a male person, fellow, chap

Blood house   a disorderly public house with a reputation for violence

Blood nut   a person with red hair

Bloody   very (the great Australian adjective)

Bloody galah   a silly person

Bloody oath!   I agree

Blotto   very drunk person

Blow   1. have a rest; 2. fail in something

Blow in   an uninvited person, stranger

Blow in the bag   breathalyser test

Blow me down   expression of surprise

Blower   a telephone

Blowie   a blowfly

Bludge   impose on one's generosity

Blowies are large, metallic coloured flies that lay their eggs on carcasses and other organic matter.

9

Bludger a very lazy person
Blue a fight
Blue-arsed fly a blue blowfly
Blue heeler an Australian cattle dog
Blue, make a make a mistake
Bluey 1. swag; 2. traffic ticket; 3. redhead
Bluey 4. blue cattle dog; 5. bluebottle jellyfish
Blue flyer female red kangaroo
Blunder a mistake
Boardies board shorts
Bobby dazzler something very good
Bob's your uncle all is well
Bodgy false, worthless
Bog going to the toilet
Bog house outside toilet
Bog in eat heartily
Bogan loutish person
Bogged vehicle stuck in the sand or mud
Boiler an old woman
Bomb 1. run-down car; 2. make a large splash when jumping into a pool
Bomb 3. fail a test; 4. something very cool; 5. spray with graffiti
Boney very thin, emaciated
Bonkers out of control, crazy
Bonnet car's front engine cover, hood
Bonzer excellent, good
Boogie board small surfboard, body board
Bookie a bookmaker
Boomer a large kangaroo
Boomerang an Aboriginal weapon
Boot car rear luggage compartment, trunk

The **bog house**, **dunny** or **thunder box** was found in most **Aussie** backyards until the mid 20th Century.

Booze   alcoholic drink

Booze bus   vehicle used for assessing a driver's blood alcohol concentration

Boozer   1. a pub or hotel; 2. a person who is a heavy drinker

Bored shitless   extremely bored

Boss cocky   an employer

Bottle shop   liquor store

Bottle-o   liquor store, bottle shop

Bottler   excellent!

Bottling, your blood's worth   a compliment of very special praise

Bouncer   a person employed to evict troublemakers

Bower bird   a collector of trash and many objects

Bozo   idiot

Brass   money, cash

Brass monkey, freeze the balls off a   very cold

Brass razoo, he hasn't got a   he is very poor

Breaker   a person who breaks in horses

Brekkie   breakfast

Brickie   a brick layer

Bring a plate   bring a plate of food to a party or barbeque

Brisvegas   Brisbane, state capital of Queensland

Brizzie   Brisbane, state capital of Queensland

Broke   no money

Brown eye   expose one's anus or bum

Brown nose   suck up to the boss, crawler, boot licker

Brumby   wild Australian horse

Bub   1. baby; 2. affectionate name for one's girlfriend or wife

Buck's night   stag party, male gathering on the eve before a wedding

Buckley's/Buckley's chance   no chance at all

Buddy   mate, pal

Budgie   budgerigar

B

Budgie smugglers   men's bathing costume
Bugger   1. person; 2. annoying person, nuisance; 3. cause inconvenience
Bugger all   very little amount
Bugger off   go away
Buggered   1. broken; 2. very tired
Built   good physique, well built
Built like a brick shit house   solidly built
Bull bar   a bar fixed to a vehicle to protect it against hitting wildlife
Bull dust   a lie
Bull shit   unbelievable statement
Bum   1. buttocks; 2. tramp; 3. get for nothing; 4. mild annoyance
Bum fluff   facial hair growth on a teenage male
Bum nuts   eggs
Bum steer   false information
Bundy   Bundaberg, Queensland and the rum that is produced there
Bung   1. damaged, broken; 2. place or put without care; 3. stopper
Bunyip   a mythical creature
Burl   try something
Burn   drive at high speed
Bush   rural Australia
Bush bash   to travel off road in a vehicle
Bushie   a person from the bush
Bushranger   an outlaw
Bush telegraph   gossip network
Bush whacker   a derogatory term for a person from the outback
Butcher   a small glass of beer in South Australia
Butcher's hook   cook or chef
By jingoes   exclamation of wonder
Cab sav   cabernet sauvignon wine
Cabbie   taxi driver

Cack   defecate
Cackelberry   egg
Cactus   broken, not working
Cadge   beg or borrow
Cagey   shy, wary
Cahoots   in partnership
Cake hole   mouth
Camp as a row of tents   a male homosexual
Camp oven   cast iron cooking pot
Can   a prison
Can of worms   problems, troublesome
Cancer stick   cigarette
Can-do   affirmative, yes
Cane toad   a person from Queensland
Caper   activity
Captain Cook   look
Carbie/Carby   carburetor
Cardie   cardigan
Cark it   to die
Carnie   carnival worker
Cash and carry   a supermarket
Cashed up   plenty of money
Chalkie   a school teacher
Champers   champagne
Chancy   uncertain, risky
Charge like a wounded bull   to charge excessively high prices
Cheese and kisses   wife
Cheesed off   very angry, annoyed
Cherry   a red cricket ball
Chew the fat   have a chat or conversation

Cooking in a **camp oven** is part of **Aussie outback** history and today the **camp oven** is used by campers.

Chewie   chewing gum
Chiack   taunt, tease
Chicken shit   no value, worthless
China plate   mate, pal, friend
Chin wag   have a chat, conversation
Chippie   a carpenter, wood worker
Chips   potato fries, crisps
Chock a block/Chockers   very full, overflowing
Chockie   chocolate
Chockie bikkies   chocolate biscuits
Choke a brown dog   something distasteful, bad food
Choof off   go now, get lost, leave
Chook   a chicken or fowl
Choppers   teeth, false teeth
Chrissie   Christmas time
Chrome dome   a bald man
Chuck   1. throw, toss; 2. vomit
Chuck a sickie   take a work sick day when you're not sick
Chuck it in   quit, give up, surrender
Chuffed   very happy
Chunder   to vomit
Clackers   false teeth
Clanger   1. a big lie; 2. a shock
Clapped out   worn out, old
Classer   a wool grader
Claytons   fake
Cleanskin   1. a bottle of wine without a label; 2. unbranded cattle
Clear as mud   confusing
Clever dick   1. a smart person; 2. a conceited person
Clicks, Klicks, K's   kilometres

Some **Aussies** still prefer to keep **chooks** in their backyards to provide **googies** rather than buy them from the grocery shop.

Clink   prison

Clobber   clothes

Clod hoppers   feet

Clucky, feeling   broody, maternal

Coat hanger   Sydney Harbour bridge

Cobber   work mate, friend, pal

Cock up   something gone wrong

Cockie   1. cockatoo; 2. farmer, grazier; 3. cockroach

Cocky's joy   golden syrup, treacle

Codger   a perculiar person, unusual

Cods   testicles

Coit   bum, anus

Coldie   a beer bottle or can

Cockies are cold-blooded pests who thrive in warm, humid conditions. They make their home wherever they find food, moisture and shelter.

Colonial goose   a boned leg of lamb seasoned with herbs and onion

Come a gutser   1. have an accident; 2. to make a mistake

Come in spinner   call for the tossing of the coins in the game of two-up

Come the raw prawn   pretend, be naive

Come to blows   start fighting

Common as dog shit   very common

Compo   workers compensation payment

Conk   nose

Conk out   engine breakdown

Conned   tricked, deceived

Cooee   a call; often used in the bush to locate lost persons

Cook   one's wife

Cooking with gas   doing very well

Cop   1. police officer; 2. obtain; 3. caught doing something wrong

Corker   something astonishing or striking

Corroboree   a ceremonial meeting of Australian Aborigines

Cossie   swimming costume

Couldn't lie straight in bed   a cheat, liar
Counter lunch/countery   pub lunch
Country cousin   a dozen, twelve
Cove   a man, bloke or chap
Cow cocky   dairy farmer
Cow of a thing   frustrating or upsetting
Crack a fat   get an erection
Crack of dawn   first light of day
Crack onto   make a pass or pursue someone romantically
Cracker   the tip of a stock whip
Cranky   angry, in a bad mood
Creamed   soundly beaten in sport
Creek   a small stream
Crikey   an expression of astonishment

Australia has two different species of **crocs**, both of which are native to tropical Queensland.

Crim   a criminal
Croak   to die
Croc   crocodile
Crook   1. unwell; 2. no good, bad, rotten
Crook as Rookwood   sick (Rookwood being a cemetery)
Cropper, came a   fall over
Crow bar   a large lever
Crow eater   a South Australian
Crown jewels   testicles
Crud   dirt, rubbish
Cruet   the head
Cubby house   a small house made for children to play in
Cunning as a shit house rat   a very cunning person
Cuppa   a cup of tea or coffee
Curly   nickname for a bald person
Cut lunch   sandwiches or pre-packed lunch

Cut snake, mad as a 1. very upset; 2. crazy
Cut the crap stop talking rubbish
Cut up 1. upset, distressed; 2. criticise
Dab hand at good at, skilled
Dacks/Daks 1. trousers, pants; 2. underpants
Dad and Dave a shave
Daddy long legs a long-legged spider
Dag 1. an amusing person; 2. dry excreta hanging from a sheep's wool
Daggy 1. untidy; 2. dirty; 3. uncool, lacking style
Dago war-time name for Italians
Daily grind monotonous work
Dakka marijuana, pot, dope
Damper bread made from flour and water usually cooked in a camp oven
Dangle to die by hanging, to hang
Dangle the carrot offer a bribe, tempt
Darl darling
Dart a cigarette
Darwin shuffle tax avoidance scheme
Darwin stubbie a very large beer bottle
Date anus
Date roller roll of toilet paper
Dazzler brilliant, good
Dead as mutton very dead
Dead beat very tired
Dead heart the arid centre of Australia
Dead horse tomato sauce
Dead marine empty beer bottle
Dead on correct
Dead ringer a close resemblance of someone else
Dead set correct, spot on, a sure thing

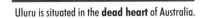

Uluru is situated in the **dead heart** of Australia.

Deadbeat 1. loser, lazy person; 2. one who doesn't pay their debts

Deadly fantastic, great, awesome

Dee a detective

Demo a demonstration

Dero/Derro a derelict, vagrant dependant on alcohol

Dial your face

Dibs marbles

Dice throw away, reject

Dicey unreliable

Dickhead jerk, annoying person, idiot

Dickory dock clock

Diddle to cheat, swindle

Diddler swindler

Dig me I've done well, excelled

Dig you you've done well, excelled

Digger an Australian soldier

Dill a stupid person

Dilly bag a small bag to carry sugar, tea, etc

Ding a minor motor accident

Ding bat a fool, silly person

Ding dong a major fight

Dinger anus, backside

Dingo an Australian native dog

Dink to carry a second person on a bike, motorcycle or horse

Dinky-di the genuine article

Dinkum no joke, the real thing

Dip out 1. miss out; 2. to refuse a drink

Dipstick idiot, a loser

Divvy up share out equally

Dob in 1. tell on someone, report; 2. contribute to a fund

The **Dingo** is **Oz's** wild dog. It is medium in size with a red to yellow coat and bushy tail. **Dingos** don't bark but they howl.

Docket   receipt, bill
Doco   a documentary
Dodgy   something suspicious
Dog and bone   phone
Dog box   a compartment in a train carriage
Dog fence   to keep dingoes out of pastoral country
Dogger   a dingo hunter
Dog's balls, stands out like   very obvious
Dog's breakfast   a real mess, confusion, turmoil
Dog's eye   a meat pie
Dole   social security payment
Dole bludger   won't work and being supported by the government
Dolled up   women dressed smartly
Done like a dinner   beaten in sport or a fight
Donga/Donger   a penis
Donk   a boat or car engine
Doodle   a penis
Doona   duvet
Doovalacky   used when you can't remember what something is called
Doover   1. a penis; 2. a thing
Dork   1. a penis; 2. someone who is uncool
Dose, a   venereal disease
Down a few   have a few drinks
Down the hatch   drink up
Down under   Australia
Drag Queen   transvestite, dresses as a woman
Drag the chain   to be slow, lag behind
Dray   a wagon, horse cart
Driza-bone   a weatherproof coat or jacket
Drongo   a stupid person

A **dog's eye** is a small meat pie often containing minced or diced meat and gravy. Sometimes smothered with **dead horse**, it is an iconic **Aussie takeaway** food snack.

Drop a fart   to pass wind
Drop kick   a useless person
Drop your guts   to fart
Drover   stock moving contractor, stockman
Drum   1. give information or advice; 2. to organise
Dry as a dead dingo's donger   very dry, thirsty
Dry rots   diarrhoea, the trots
Duchess   dressing table, sideboard
Duck's guts   a very good thing
Duckshove   pass responsibilities off to others
Dudds   male clothing
Duff   1. mess up; 2. steal cattle
Duff, up the   pregnant
Duffer   stupid person, unthinking
Duffing   stealing cattle or sheep
Dummy, spit the   have a tantrum
Dump   1. poorly kept house; 2. act of defecation; 3. end a relationship
Dumper   a large wave breaking onto a beach
Dunny   a toilet; indoor or outdoor
Dunny diver   a plumber
Dunny paper   toilet paper
Durry   a cigarette
Dust up   brawl or fight
Dutch oven   farting under the bed sheets
Dux   top of the class
Eager beaver   a keen person
Eagle eyes   very good eyesight
Eagle hawking   plucking wool from dead sheep
Eagle shits   getting paid
Ear bashing   persistent talking, nagging

Toilet paper is referred to as **dunny paper** however, in the early days, most **dunny paper** was actually torn up sheets of newspaper.

Earful   1. oral advice; 2. stern reprimand
Early bird   1. get up early; 2. arrive early
Early mark   leave work before normal finishing time
Earn a quid   working for a living, making money
Ears flapping   eavesdropping, listening in
Easy   1. to have no firm preference; 2. promiscuous
Easy lay   a woman with loose morals
Easy-peasy   very easy
Eat a horse   very hungry
Eat a horse and chase the rider   indicating one's great hunger
Eat crow   embarrassment when a plan has failed or backfired
Edgy   nervous
Egg beater   helicopter
Egg head   an intellectual person
Ekka   the Brisbane Agricultural Exhibition
Elbow grease   hard work
El-cheapo   1. something very cheap; 2. inferior quality
Elevator   lift
Emcee   master of ceremony
Empties   empty beer bottles
Emu   a racecourse person who picks up discarded betting tickets
Emu-bobber   someone employed to pick up rubbish after a function
Emu parade   group of people employed to clean up after large gatherings
Entree   appetiser, starter
Enzed/NZ   an acronym, New Zealand
Enzedder   a New Zealander
Esky   a portable insulated container used to keep food and drink cool
Even stevens   1. equal; 2. not owed anything
Even the score   revenge
Every dog has its day   opportunities come your way

Every man and his dog   a general public crowd
Every Tom, Dick and Harry   a general public crowd
Every which way   all directions
Ex   one's former wife, husband, girlfriend or boyfriend
Exchange notes   to gossip
Excuse the French   apology for bad language
Expecting   pregnant
Exy   expensive

Eye off   to look at with interest

Every Tom, Dick and Harry was at the opening of the new shopping centre.

Eyeball to eyeball   face to face
Eyes like road maps   bloodshot after a big night out
Eyesore   offensive, ugly
FJ   a popular model of the Holden car 1953-1956
Fab   fabulous, wonderful, great
Face ache   irritating person
Face fungus   a beard
Face like a festered pimple   1. acute acne; 2. ugly
Face, off one's   drunk
Fag   1. a cigarette; 2. a homosexual
Fagged out   tired
Fair and square   honest, trustworthy
Fair crack of the whip   to be treated fairly, asking for a fair chance
Fair dinkum   real, true
Fair enough   agreeing about something
Fair go mate   give a chance
Fair suck of the sav   1. a fair go; 2. exclamation of wonder or disbelief
Fairy   homosexual male
Fairy floss   cotton candy, candy floss
Falsies   1. fake breasts; 2. false teeth
Famished   very hungry

Fangs teeth
Fanny a vagina
Far flung remote, far away
Fart sack 1. a bed or bunk; 2. a sleeping bag
Fart-arse waste time
Farts like a two-stroke loud flatulence
Fat cake damper fried in fat
Favourite poison preferred alcoholic drink
Feel crook unwell
Feel horny sexually aroused
Fell off the back of a truck stolen property
Fella a male person
Feral a hippie
Fergie/Fergy a Ferguson tractor
Ferret a penis
Few and far between rare, not common
Fib a lie, untruth
Fibber a liar
Fiddle to cheat
Fiddler a swindler

Feral Meryl believes the way to peace is through love and tolerance.

Fifty-fifty equal amounts
Figjam *uck I'm good just ask me; high opinion of oneself
Filly 1. a young girl; 2. female horse
Filthy rich very wealthy
Finicky fastidious
Fins the arms
Fire away begin to speak
Fire blanks a sterile male
Firebug arsonist
First cab off the rank first in line

First fleeter   a person who can be traced back to the first fleet
First thing   early morning
Fish out of water   uncomfortable with other people or surroundings
Fisho   a fishmonger
Fit as a mallee bull   a very fit person
Fits like a glove   suitable, a good fit
Five o'clock shadow   beard growth on a man's face
Five finger discount   shop lifting
Fizzer   1. a failure; 2. fiasco
Flak   criticism
Flake   shark's flesh; commonly sold in fish and chip shops
Flake out   lie down, to sleep
Flame   girlfriend, sweetheart
Flamin'   1. very good; 2. very bad
Flap your gums   talk too much
Flash a brown eye   expose ones bare backside, anus
Flasher   a man who exposes his genitals in public

Fred the **flasher.**

Flat as a tack   1. tired, worn out; 2. anything that is flat
Flat broke   having no money
Flat chat   as fast as possible
Flat out like a lizard drinking   a very busy person, working hard
Flatfoot   a policeman
Flatties   low-heeled shoes
Flea bag   infested with fleas
Flea-house   cinema, picture theatre
Flesh and blood   family, kin, offspring
Flick   1. getting rid of something; 2. movie
Flick it on   sell something soon after buying for a quick profit
Flippers   hands
Floater   1. a meat pie in a plate of gravy; 2. faeces floating in a toilet

Flog   1. to sell something; 2. to steal something

Flogging a dead horse   trying to do something when it won't work

Floozie   a promiscuous woman

Fluke   to win by chance

Flunk   to fail

Flutter   place a small bet

Fly the coop   1. escape; 2. leave home

Flyblown   maggots on meat

Flying fox   a cable car

Fob off   1. dismiss; 2. be rude to someone

Foggiest   no idea or clue

Snowy took **forty winks** during **smoko** because he couldn't keep his **peepers** open.

Fool's gold   pyrites; a mineral that resembles gold

Foot the bill   pay the costs

Footpath   sidewalk

Footslogger   a soldier

Footy   term for Australian rules football, rugby league or rugby union

For keeps   permanently own

Fork over   pay a bet, hand over something

Forty winks   a short nap or sleep

Fossick   search for gold or gemstones

Fossil   an old person

Foulmouthed   using obscene language

Four eyes   a person who wears glasses

Four letter word   any vulgar words having four letters

Four-b-two/four   a piece of timber

Foursome   four people in a party

Franger   a condom

Freckle   the anus

Fred Nerk   an imaginary person

Free loader   a person who uses somebody's hospitality, food and drink

Freebie   something for nothing
Free-for-all   a fight involving many people
Freeze the balls off a brass monkey   very cold, frosty
Fremantle Doctor   Perth breeze from the direction of Fremantle
Frenchie   a condom
Freo   Fremantle, Western Australia
Freshie   a fresh water crocodile
Fridge   a refrigerator
Fried eggs   flat breasts
Frig   to masturbate
Frigging   masturbating
Frigid   an unresponsive person
Frillie   a frill-necked lizard
Fringe benefit   extra rewards above regular wage
Frisky   sexually aroused
Frog   a French person
Frog and toad   road
Frogshit   insincere talk, nonsense
From a to z   from the beginning to the end
From arsehole to breakfast time   1. all over; 2. completely covered
From go to whoa   from the beginning to the end
From pillar to post   roaming from one place to another
From scratch   from nothing
Fruit for the sideboard   perks, rewards, bonus
Fruitloop   a crazy person
Fuddy-duddy   1. conservative; 2. a fussy person
Full as a boot   very drunk, intoxicated
Full bore   to go all out
Full frontal   a naked body from front on
Full of beans   very energetic

The **fridge** was absolutely **chockers** with drinks and **tucker**.

Full of shit   talking rubbish

Full on   most intense

Full quid   sane

Fungus face   a male with a beard

Furphy   1. originally a water cart; 2. a rumour or a false report, a lie

Fuss pot   1. a person who worries a lot; 2. a very fussy person

Fuzz   the police

Fuzzy-headed   a bad hangover

Fuzzy wuzzy angel   WWII stretcher bearer from Papua New Guinea

G'day/Gidday   Good-day, hello

Ga Ga   mad, silly

Gab   chatter, talk

Gabba   Queensland Cricket Ground at Wooloongabba, Brisbane

Gadabout   a person having an active social life

Gag   a joke

Galah   1. native Australian parrot; 2. a fool, idiot

Gallops   thoroughbred horse races

Galoot   a stupid clumsy person

Galvo   galvanized iron

Game as a piss ant   a very daring person

Game as Ned Kelly   very daring

Games up   the end of an activity

Gammy   crippled, lame

Gander   have a look at something

Gangie   group sex

Ganja   marijuana

Gaol bird   habitual criminal

Garbage guts   a greedy person

Garbo   garbage or waste collector

Gas bagging   talk at great length non-stop.

Ned Kelly is an **Aussie** folk hero yet he was a criminal. He is remembered today in the popular expression, "as **game as Ned Kelly**".

Gasper a cigarette
Gawk stare openly
Gear clothes, uniform
Gee gee a horse
Geek have a look
Genny a generator
Gents a public toilet for men only
German band your hand
Get a bit have sexual intercourse
Get a dose contract a venereal disease
Get a leg in the door make headway
Get a wriggle on hurry up
Get nicked exclamation of contempt
Get off at Redfern withdraw before ejaculation
Get rooted a term of abuse; go away!
Get stuffed a term of abuse; go away, piss off!
Get stuck into 1. abuse someone; 2. eat hungrily; 3. do a task with vigour
Get the arse to be fired/sacked
Get the big A to be fired/sacked
Get the nod get approval, the go ahead
Get the rough end of the pineapple worst treatment
Get the shits get upset
Gibber a round stone, a small rock
Gig 1. performance at a venue; 2. gigabyte
Gimme give me
Give the game away to abandon interest
Give it a burl to try, have a go
Give it a miss change one's mind
Give lip cheeky, answer back
Glad rags your best clothes

Jo and Flo spent most of the day **gas bagging** about the new **bloke** at the office.

Glass of amber   a glass of beer
Go ape shit   become very angry
Go bad   1. down on one's luck; 2. a bad joke that is not appreciated
Go down like a lead balloon   failure
Go Dutch   pay your own way
Go for a burn   1. to drive fast; 2. test drive
Go for a snake hiss   a male to urinate
Go like the clappers   move fast
Go off half-cocked   not thinking straight
Go to buggery   ask someone to leave in a very nasty way
Go walkabout   wandering off
Goanna   a piano
Gob   mouth
Gobful, give a   to abuse
Gobsmacked   astounded, flabbergasted
Goer   1. an energetic person; 2. go ahead with something
Going off   used to describe a fun night spot or party
Gone to billyo   disappeared
Gone to the dogs   going from good to bad
Good as gold   something very good
Good monger   good food
Good oil   correct information
Good on ya   well done
Good sort   a good looking woman
Goog, as full as a   1. drunk; 2. full of food
Googie   an egg
Goolies   testicles
Goss   gossip
Grab forty winks   have a nap
Grazier   pastoral property owner

Nothing beats a boiled **googie** for **brekkie**.

Greasy   a bad cook

Great Australian salute   the action of shooing flies away with your hand

Green around the gills   feeling sick

Green thumb   able to make any plant grow

Greenie   an environmentalist

Grizzle   to complain

Grog   alcohol

Grommet   a teenage surfer

Grot   an untidy person

Grouse   very good, terrific

Grub   1. food; 2. a meal; 3. a dirty eater; 4. a dirty child

Grundies   underwear (from television and media mogul, Reg Grundy)

Grunt   power, strength

Gully   a very small valley

Gummies   gumboots

Gun   1. best at something; 2. accelerate a vehicle

Gunna   all talk and no action

Gunyah   an aboriginal shelter

Gutful   had enough

Gutful of piss   drunk

Gutsy   brave, fearsome

Guttersnipe   a gossiper

Gutzer   to fall over, trip

Guzzler   a heavy drinker

Gyno   a gynecologist

Barry **hoed into** a big plate of **grub** for **tea**.

Hack   1. a taxi; 2. horse

Had a few too many   too many alcoholic drinks

Had a good innings   a good life

Had a skin full   drinks too much

Had it   1. run out of patience; 2. dead

Had it soft   an easy time

Hair of the dog   a drink to cure a hangover

Half shot   nearly intoxicated

Half time   the middle of a team sport's game

Half your luck   very lucky

Half-mast   trousers that don't reach the ankles

Ham and eggs   legs

Hammer and tongs   worked very hard

Hammy   hamstring

Hand   a hired worker

Hand in hand   worked together

Hand in the till   stealing from employer

Hand the hat around   giving to a cause

Hand-me-downs   passed on clothing

Handy   skilled, clever

Hang around like a bad smell   not wanted around

Hang on a tick   wait a minute

Hanger-on   a free loader

Hankie   handkerchief

Happy as a pig in shit   very happy

Happy as Larry   extremely happy

Happy little vegemite   someone in a good mood

Hard word on   1. to ask a favour; 2. to ask a sexual favour

Hassle   1. a problem; 2. inconvenience

Hate someone's guts   dislike someone

Haul   ill gotten goods

Haunt   favourite place

Have a ball   a very good time

Have a bang   have sexual intercourse

Have a barney   a fight

Have a bo-peep   have a look
Have a burl   attempt something
Have a crack   attempt
Have a decko/dekko   have a look
Have a domestic   a family argument
Have a flutter   a small bet, wager
Have a gander   have a look
Have a go   try something
Have a heart   have mercy
Have a pash   long, passionate kiss
Have a prang   car smash, accident
Have a shot at   to try something
Have a snort   have an alcoholic drink
Have a spell   a rest from work
Have a splash   have a bet, wager
Have a stab at   attempt something
Have a tub   bath or wash

Bluey decided to **have a tub** to soothe his aching body after a day of hard **yakka**.

Have long arms and short pockets   to be a miser, stingy
Haven't got a brass razoo   broke, no money
Hayburner   a horse
Head in the sand   to ignore reality
Heads and tails   used in the game of two-up
Heaps   a lot, a large amount
Heard it all before   same thing over and over
Heart of gold   1. generous; 2. helpful
Heart of stone   mean, unemotional
Heart starter   early morning alcoholic drink, strong coffee, first cigarette
Heart stopper   shocking, terrifying
Heavies   minders, bodyguards
Heebie-jeebies   tension, nervousness

Heifers   young female cattle
Hell for leather   fast, speeding
Hemp   marijuana
Hen-pecked   dominated by a wife
Hen's night   bachelorette party
Hen's teeth   scarce
Here to stay   permanent
Herk   vomit
Hey   greeting
Hick   country person
Hickey   a love bite
Hidey hole   a secret hiding place
High and dry   abandoned, alone
High as a kite   1. under the influence of drugs or alcohol; 2. in high spirits
High flying   doing well in business
High on the nose   stinking, smelly
Highfaluting   snobbish, pompous, pretentious
His nibs   the boss, one in charge
Hit and giggle   tennis
Hit and miss   careless
Hit the frog and toad   depart
Hit the hay   go to bed
Hit the headlines   achieve fame
Hit the jackpot   very lucky
Hit the nail on the head   exactly right
Hit the piss   drink heavily
Hit the roof   become angry
Hit the sack   go to bed
Hit the slops   get on the booze
Hit the toe   depart, go

Jack **hit the slops** every night at his local **watering hole** before heading home to **cop** an **ear bashing** from the **ball and chain**.

Hiya greeting

Hobbles straps used to tie horses' legs

Hoe into start eating

Hold the reins be in charge

Hollies/Hols holidays

Holy dooley exclamation indicating surprise, indignation

Holy mackerel exclamation indicating surprise, indignation

Holy smoke exclamation indicating surprise, indignation

Home and hosed easy winner; foregone conclusion, successful finish

Homely 1. plain; 2. cosy, snug

Homestead the main house on a property

Homo a homosexual man

Honk 1. the nose; 2. blow a car's horn

Honkers Hong Kong

Hooch marijuana

Hoof it to walk, run

Hooks fingers

Hooley a wild party

Hoon a reckless show off

Hoop a jockey

Hooray 1. goodbye; 2. pleasure

Hooroo goodbye

Hop it go away

Hopping mad very angry

Hops beer

Horn 1. an erection; 2. a telephone

Horn in enter a discussion uninvited

Horse and cart a fart

Horse around play up

Horse sense common sense

Bazza was **hopping mad** when he noticed that some **galoot** had **pranged** into the side of his new car.

Horse play rough behaviour

Horses for courses suited to the task

Horse's hoof homosexual

Hostie air hostess, flight attendant

Hot air pretentious, empty talk

Hot to trot eager to start

Hot foot it go, depart, leave

Hot pants a woman with strong sexual desires

Hot under the collar very angry

Hotel a pub

Hottie 1. a hot water bottle; 2. a sexy person

House of ill fame a brothel

How about it? asking for sex

How come? why

How ya goin? greeting

How's it going? greeting

How's things? greeting

Howzat? an appeal for approval

Hoy attract attention

According to **every Tom, Dick and Harry**, Brenda was a **bloody bonzer hostie** and a real **hottie**.

Hubby husband

Huey another name for God, the powers above

Humbug 1. a striped lolly; 2. a cheat

Humdinger very good, the best

Hump 1. carry something; 2. lift; 3. have sex

Humpy a rough bush shelter

Hung over feeling poorly after a drinking binge

Hurl vomit

Husband beater a rolling pin

Hush money a bribe

Hush up keep quiet

Hustle   to obtain money illegally
Hype   overdone
Hyped up/Hypo   over excited
I.O.U   "I owe you", a written confirmation of debt
I kid you not   declaration that one is speaking the truth
I'll be   exclamation of surprise
I'll drink to that   agree, approve
I'm all right Jack   ok
I've had it   complete frustration
Ice block/Icy pole   popsicle
Icing on the cake   best finish
Icky   1. offensive; 2. risky
Idiot box   a television set
Idle rich   very wealthy people
Iffy   suspicious
Illywhacker   a small time trickster, crook
Imp   a naughty child
In a jiff/jiffy   soon, a short time
In a spin   confused
In a spot of bother   in trouble
In a tic   soon
In cloudland   not concentrating
In cog   in disguise, incognito
In droves   big numbers
In fine feathers   full of vitality
In fits and starts   irregular
In for the kill   defeat
In good nick   good condition
In hock   in debt
In house   associated to members of a house or club

An **ice block** is a sweet cold confection consisting of ice cream or flavoured water frozen on a stick.

In like Flynn   1. a sure thing; 2. sexual success (referring to Errol Flynn)

In strife   in trouble

In the bag   success

In the box seat   successful position

In the can   in prison

In the chair   next to buy a round of drinks

In the clink   in gaol

In the cooler   in gaol

In the cot   in bed

In the doghouse   out of favour with your wife, husband or partner

In the drink   in water

In the family way   pregnant

In the good books   in favour

In the grip of the grape   addicted to wine

In the guts   in the centre, middle

In the know   inside information

In the nuddy   naked

In the raw   naked, nude

In the red   in debt

In the right place at the right time   in a good position

In the same boat   in the same situation, face the same challenges

In the shit   in serious trouble

In the sticks   remote areas in the bush

In the wars   1. minor injuries; 2. arguments

In tow   following someone

In trouble   pregnant

Indian giver   give a gift to someone then take it back

Info   information

In-laws   relatives by marriage

Inside job   a crime within an organisation

Into thin air   disappear
Intro   introduction
Irish curtains   cobwebs
Iron clad   safe
Iron fisted   ruthless, severe
Iron oneself out   get drunk
Iron underpants   girdles, step-ins
Irrits   the shits
Is it a goer?   will it happen?
Is the Pope Catholic?   yes
It   could be male or female

Yes, the Pope is Catholic.

It's a goer   1. will happen; 2. proceed
It's in the cards   may happen
It's sweet   all is ok
It's your funeral   your fault
It never rains but it pours   lots of things happen at once
Itchy feet   need to travel
Itsy-bitsy   very small, tiny
Ivories   teeth, false teeth
J.P.   a Justice of the Peace
Jab   an injection
Jabber   to talk rapidly
Jack dancer   cancer
Jack in the box   someone who cannot sit still
Jack of all trades   someone who can do all jobs
Jacked off   1. annoyed; 2. disgusted; 3. frustrated
Jack Shay   to stay
Jack shit   nothing
Jack up   1. refuse to work; 2. disobey
Jackass   1. kookaburra; 2. an idiot

Jacked off   1. annoyed; 2. masturbated

Jackeroo   a male stock hand

Jackie/Jacky   kookaburra

Jacky Howe   a sleeveless garment worn by labourers

Jaffle   a toasted sandwich

Jake   okay, alright

Jam tart   sweetheart

Jammed in   over-crowded

Jargon   nonsense, meaningless talk

Jarmies   pyjamas, night dress

Jay-cee   Jesus Christ

Jelly   1. gelatin desert, jello; 2. gelignite, explosive

Jerk   a fool

Jerkin the gherkin   to masturbate

Jerry built   badly built

Jiffy   very short time

Jiggered   broken, spoiled

Jillaroo   a female stock hand

Jimmy Woodser   a person who drinks on their own in a bar

Jingoes   exclamation of surprise

Jittery   nervous, anxious

Job somebody   to hit someone, fight

Jock   genital support worn by sportsmen

Jockeys   male underpants

Jocks   male underpants

Joe Blake   a snake

Joe Bloggs   anybody

Joe Blow   an ordinary bloke

Joey   baby kangaroo

John   1. a policeman; 2. a toilet; 3. prostitute's client

Johnny cake   1. damper; 2. bush cakes
Johnny come lately   a recent arrival
Join up   enlist for military service
Joint   a house, place, abode
Joker   1. a person who is amusing; 2. a person you're unsure about
Jollies   sexual excitement
Jonah   to bring bad luck
Journo   a journalist
Joy ride   an enjoyable ride
Jug   1. prison; 2. measure of beer served in a large glass jug
Juggle the pennies   budget
Jugs   breasts, boobs
Juice   petrol, gas
Jumble sale   a sale of second-hand items
Jumbuck   a sheep
Jump at it   1. chance it; 2. offered a job
Jump bail   abscond after paying bail
Jump in and out of bed   be very promiscuous
Jump in the lake   go away, piss off
Jump start   get a good start
Jump the gun   start too soon
Jump the queue   jump in front of someone in line
Jump the rattler   ride the train illegally
Jumper   1. sweater, pullover; 2. commit suicide by jumping from a height
Jump up and down   1. make a fuss; 2. strongly protest
Jumpy   nervous, tense
Jungle juice   home-made inferior alcoholic drink
Junk   anything that is worthless
Junk food   take-away food
Jump the gun   gain an unfair advantage by starting prematurely

Jumbuck is an **Aussie** term for sheep and is featured in the famous poem and song, "Waltzing Matilda".

Just down the street   not far away
Just my luck   frustration
Just what the doctor ordered   exactly what is required
K's   kilometres
Kafuffle   a commotion
Kamikaze   a reckless act
Kanaka   a Pacific Islander (seldom used)
Kanakas   testicles
Kanga   1. kangaroo; 2. shoe
Kaput   1. broken, smashed; 2. is dead
Kark   1. die; 2. broken, ruined
Keel over   1. to fall over; 2. die; 3. faint
Keen as mustard   very enthusiastic
Keen on someone   attracted to someone
Keep a low profile   keep away from publicity
Keep an eye on everything   watch over, look after
Keep back   restrain, withhold
Keep in touch   maintain a friendship
Keep it in the family   keep secrets within a family
Keep on the ball   constant alertness
Keep one's chin up   maintain good spirits, courage
Keep one's head above water   survive at all costs
Keep one's mouth shut   refrain from speaking out
Keep your shirt on   settle down, take it easy
Keg   a barrel of beer
Kelpie   an Australian sheepdog
Kero   kerosene
Khyber pass   arse, bum
Kick   1. pleasurable thrill; 2. strong alcohol taste; 3. trouser pocket
Kick arse   totally amazing

Kick back   relax
Kick in   1. to contribute; 2. buy a drink
Kick in the arse   a severe scolding
Kick in the teeth   a severe setback
Kick off   commence to play sport; football, soccer
Kick on   to continue
Kick the bucket   to die
Kick the tin   1. donate; 2. buy a round of drinks
Kick up one's heels   have fun
Kiddo   to address a young person
Kicking up a shinty   making an angry fuss
Kill a brown dog   potent, deadly
Kill a snake   urinate
Kill the goose that lays the golden eggs   end something profitable
Killer, a   a sheep or cow killed for meat on a property
Kimberley cool   the coolness beer reaches when immersed in a water bag
Kimberley formal   men's dress style; shirt, shorts, socks and shoes
Kimberley mutton   wild goat roasted
Kindie   kindergarten
King Dick   1. the best; 2. above ordinary people
King hit   a surprise punch in the head
King pin   a boss or leader
Kink   1. a cramp, twinge; 2. a sexual pervert
Kinky   unusual sexual tastes
Kip   1. a small thin piece of flat wood used to toss coins in a game of two-up
Kip   2. a short sleep
Kiwi   a New Zealander
Klicks   kilometres
Knackered   very tired
Knackers   testicles

Knee high to a grasshopper   a short person

Knee trembler   1. frightening; 2. sexual intercourse standing up

Knickers   underpants for women

Knick knacks   trinkets, bric a brac

Knife in the back   a betrayal

Knob   1. penis; 2. annoying or stupid person, dickhead

Knock   to criticise

Knock back   1. a refusal, a rebuff; 2. consume a drink

Knock down   1. reduce the price; 2. spend freely on liquor

Knock it off   1. stop it!; 2. euphemism for sexual intercourse

Knock off   1. stop work; 2. steal something; 3. make a copy

Knock shop   a brothel

Knock up   1. make pregnant; 2. construct; 3. cook hastily; 4. exhaust

Knocked up   pregnant

Knocker   one who derides all ideas, things and projects

Knuckle down   show willing to work

Knuckle sandwich   a bunch of fives, a punch to the teeth

Knuckle, to go the   to fight, to punch

Kombi   a small van, wagon

Konk   nose

Koori   an aborigine

Kosher   the real thing

Kybosh   rubbish, nonsense

Lab   laboratory

Lace into   attack, abuse

Ladies   womens' toilet

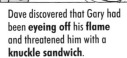

Dave discovered that Gary had been **eyeing off** his **flame** and threatened him with a **knuckle sandwich**.

Ladies man   a man attracted to women

Lady muck   a snobby woman

Lady's waist   either a 5 or 7 ounce glass of beer

Lag   a habitual criminal, convict

Lagerphone a musical instrument made of bottle tops nailed to a stick

Lagger a police informer

Laid up sick, bedridden

Laid back relaxed

Lair/Lairy 1. a flashy male; 2. vulgar person; 3. show off

Lamington small square sponge cake coated in chocolate icing and coconut

Lappy a laptop

Larrikin a prankster, hooligan

Lash at, have a to make an attempt at something

Lash out 1. spend freely; 2. burst into violent action or criticise severely

Last resort a final option

Laugh at the lawn to vomit

Laughing gear the mouth

Laughing jackass a kookaburra

Lav/Lavvy outdoor toilet, any toilet

Lay a person considered as a sex object, a good lay

Lay a cable to defecate

Lay down the law what I say goes, the boss

Lay in the hay have sexual intercourse

Lay into to beat up, abuse

Lay low stay out of site

Lay off 1. ease up, stop; 2. be sacked

Layabout a lazy person

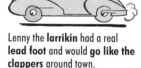

Lenny the **larrikin** had a real **lead foot** and would **go like the clappers** around town.

Lay-down misere it's a certainty

Lazy Susan a revolving centre tray on a dining table

Lead a dog's life an unhappy life

Lead feet/foot to drive too fast, a reckless driver

Leak to urinate

Learner a person learning to drive a motor vehicle

Leave it at that end of story, say no more in conversation

Left to the wolves   deserted

Left footer   a Catholic

Leg it   to walk or run

Legal eagle   a lawyer or solicitor

Legless   very drunk

Lemon   1. shoddy work; 2. a faulty car

Lend of, to have a   take advantage of a gullible person

Lezzo/Lesbo   a Lesbian

Let 'er rip   an enthusiastic start of something

Let one's hair down   behave in an informal manner

Let sleeping dogs lie   cause no further trouble

Let slip   to reveal a secret

Lick into shape   repair, fix up

Lick the dust   to die or be wounded

Licked   to be beaten or defeated

Lid   a hat

Lie doggo   1. to hide away; 2. get out of something

Lie in   stay in bed, get up late

Lie low   stay out of site

Life of Riley   a trouble free existence

Light on   horse racing short weight

Like a shag on a rock   1. a loner; 2. out of place

Like buggery   no way

Like the clappers   very fast

Line 'em up   lining up a round of drinks

Lingo   language

Lippy   lipstick

Lizard drinking, flat out like a   very busy

Loaded   1. very wealthy; 2. under the effects of alcohol or drugs, stoned

Lob/Lob in   1. arrive unannounced; 2. drop in to see someone

Lollies   candy, sweets
Longneck   750ml bottle of beer in South Australia
Lucky country, the   Australia
Lug   1. carry; 2. ear; 3. clumsy person
Lurk   1. underhanded racket; 2. scheme; 3. on to a good thing
Mad as a cut snake   crazy, insane
Mad as a meat axe   extremely mad
Mag   magazine
Maggie   magpie
Maidenhood   virginity
Make a blue   make a mistake, error
Make a quid   earn a living, wage, salary
Make it snappy   hurry up
Make tracks   depart, leave
Make waves   to cause trouble
Makings, the   tobacco and cigarette papers, to roll your own
Malarky   foolish talk, raving on, idle gossip
Mallee   unpopulated scrub or bushland
Mallee bull, fit as a   very strong, fit
Man in white   a cricket umpire
Man on the land   a farmer or grazier
Manchester   household linen
Man's best friend   1. his dog; 2. his penis
Manual   a car with a manual gear shift
March down the aisle   to get married
Marching orders   getting the sack, to be fired
Marge   margarine
Marriage on the rocks   a marriage break up
Marties   tomatoes
Mary's room   the toilet

"The Lucky Country" is a nickname used to describe Australia, taken from the 1964 book by the same name by social critic Donald Horne.

Mash   mashed potatoes
Mate   close friend
Mate's rate   cheaper than usual price for a friend
Matilda   a blanket roll, a swag
Metho   methylated spirits
Middy   a 10 ounce glass of beer (NSW and Western Australia)
Mike   a microphone
Milk bar   corner store that usually sells take-away food
Milko   milkman
Mince pies   the eyes
Min-min light   a strange light that appears in outback Queensland
Missus, the   a man's spouse, wife
Mite   a small child, infant
Mitt   a hand or fist
Mo   moustache
Mob   1. cattle or sheep herd; 2. group of people
Mog/Moggy   a cat
Molly dooker   a left-handed person
Money bags   a rich person
Mongrel   1. mixed-breed dog; 2. despicable person; 3. something difficult
Moniker   a person's name
Monkey suit   a dinner suit
Moo   a silly woman
Moo juice   milk
Moolah   cash, money
Moosh   mouth
Mozzie   a mosquito
Muddie   a Queensland mud crab
Mudmap   a map or a sketch drawn on the ground
Muff   female genitals

Mug 1. face; 2. one who is easily fooled; 3. friendly insult
Mulga the outback bush
Mullock spoil or rock tailings from a mine
Munga food
Murphy a potato
Mushie a mushroom
Muso a musician
Muster to herd or gather cattle or sheep
Mutt a mongrel dog
Mutton head a foolish person
My oath total agreement
Mystery bags sausages or snags

Bevan was a **muso** with **bloody** big dreams but spent most of his life **flat broke.**

Myxo myxomatosis, viral disease introduced to deplete rabbit population
NBG no bloody good
NRL National rugby league
Nab arrest, capture
Nada 1. nothing, zero, zip; 2. free
Nag 1. old inferior horse; 2. talk incessantly
Nail 1. catch, seize; 2. kill; 3. do something perfectly
Nail-biter an exciting match or game with a close finish
Nana/Narna a banana
Nanna/Nanny/Nannie grandmother
Nappy diaper
Nark a person who nags and irritates continually
Narky short-tempered
Nasho national serviceman
Natter chat, gossip
Naughty, have a have sex
Near-at-hand close by
Neato excellent, great

Neddies   racing horses
Never never   desert regions of Australia
New chum   1. a newcomer; 2. beginner
Newbie   a newcomer to anything
Newsagent   a shop where you buy newspapers, magazines and books
Nibbles   a snack, small tit-bits of food
Nice drop   a good wine
Nick   to steal
Nick off   depart, go away
Nickers   women's underpants
Nigel   unpopular person, has no friends
Niggly   annoyed, angry
Night on the town   a big night out
Nineteenth hole   a bar in the golf club house
Nipper   1. a small crab or prawn; 2. a young child; 3. a young surf lifesaver
Nippy   1. cold; 2. active person
Nitwit   foolish person
No drama   no problem
No hoper   a fool, a person without merit
No room to swing a cat   a small room, cramped quarters
No worries   no problem
Nob   1. annoying person; 2. head; 3. elite person
Nod off   to fall asleep, have a nap
Noggin   the head
Nong   an idiot
Nope   no
Norks   breasts
North and South   mouth
Nosebag   meal, feed
Nosh   food

Nosh up   1. very big meal; 2. to eat
Nosey parker   stickybeak
Not a bad old stick   a good person
Not bad   good, excellent
Not for quids   no way
Not much chop   not good, below standards
Not on your Nellie   no way
Not the full quid   insane, stupid
Nothing between the ears   a foolish or stupid person
Nous   common sense
Nozzle   the nose
Nuddy   in the nude
Nugget   a stocky thickset person
Nuggety   a stocky thickset person, solidly built
Nulla-nulla   an aboriginal club, weapon
Numb skull   fool, idiot
Numbnuts   ineffectual man
Numbskull   dim-witted person, fool, idiot
Nut   1. head; 2. eccentric or insane person; 3. enthusiast; 4. testicle
Nut case   1. eccentric person; 2. crazy person
Nut chokers   mens' underwear, briefs, underpants
Nut house   an asylum
Nut out   work out, solve a problem
Nutted   castrated
Nympho   a nymphomaniac
O.P.   overproof as in rum
O.S.   overseas
Oath!   definitely; yes!
Obs   objections
Ocean-going   any seaworthy vessel

Ocker   1. stereotypical uncultured Australian; 2. destinctively Australian
Ockerism   referring to the ocker character
Odd jobs   casual work
Off colour   sick, unwell
Off like a bride's nightie   1. quickly remove clothing; 2. departed quickly
Off like a rocket   1. successful event; 2. depart quickly
Offsider   1. an assistant; 2. partner
Oi   hey you
Oinker   a pig
Okey dokey   things are good, okay
Old biddy   an old women
Old bomb   a dilapidated vehicle
Old codger   an old man
Old coot   an old person
Old fella   penis
Old flame   a lover from the past
Old fogey   an old-fashioned person
Oldies   aged parents
On a bender   drinking to excess
On a sticky wicket   in trouble
On the blink   broken down, not working
On the blower   on the phone
On the bludge   cadging money
On the cuff   on credit
On the dole   receiving social security benefits whilst unemployed
On the grog   drinking alcohol in excess
On the house   free drinks
On the level   honest
On the nose   smelly
On ya   good on you, well done

Greg spent all day **on the blower** trying to track down the **old codger** who left his **jumper** on the bus.

On your bike   get out of here, go
On your Pat Malone   on your own, alone
One and all   everybody
One and only   unique
One-arm bandit   a poker machine
One for the road   last drink
One tonner   a small truck, utility
One-eyed trouser snake   a penis
Oodles   large quantities
Op   1. surgical operation; 2. operator
Op shop   opportunity shop selling second hand goods
Optic nerve   a perve
Out cold   unconscious
Out of it   1. incapacitated as a result of alcohol or drugs; 2. spaced out
Outback   inland Australia, sparsely settled
Outstation   remote from main homestead
Over the hill   getting old
Overland trout   a goanna, lizard
Overlander   one who droves stock over long distances
Ow   sudden pain
Own up   admit, confess
Ow-ya-goin?   how are you?
Oz   Australia, an Australian
Ozzie   an Australian person
PJ's   pyjamas
Pack death   to be very afraid, scared
Pack it in   to quit
Paddo   Paddington, a suburb in Sydney and Brisbane
Paddock   an area of land enclosed by a fence
Panties   woman's underpants

The **one arm bandit** was operated by a lever on the side but today's **pokies** are operated by buttons on the front panel.

Parson's nose the tail of a cooked chicken

Party pooper a person who spoils a party

Pash a kiss and cuddle

Pass away to die

Pass round the hat take up a collection

Pass wind to fart

Passion pit a drive in cinema

Pat Malone on your own, alone

Pav a pavlova; sweet meringue dessert cake

Payback retaliatory action taken according to tribal code by aborigines

Pea soup a thick fog

Pearler something very good

Pearlies teeth

Pecking order social standing

Pee urinate

Peepers eyes

Pegs 1. legs; 2. teeth

Perve one person lustfully eyeing another person

Petrol head a person obsessed by his or her car

Piccaninny an aboriginal child, baby

Picker up a person who picks up the shorn fleeces in the sheering shed

Piddle to urinate

Piece of piss quite simple

Pig rooting a horse bucking

Pig's arse highly unlikely

Piker one who leaves early, pulls out of a situation

Pink slip, get the get the sack, fired; lose one's job

Pinny an apron

Pins legs

Pint large glass of beer mainly in South Australia

Piss   1. to urinate; 2. alcohol
Piss head   drunkard
Piss off   depart, leave
Piss pot   an alcoholic, heavy drinker
Plate, bring a   bring a plate of food to a party or barbeque
Plates of meat   feet
Plodder   a slow worker
Plonk   very cheap wine
Pocket billiards   hands in pockets and play with genitals
Pointing Percy at the porcelain   to urinate
Pokies   poker machines
Pollies   politicians
Pommy   a British subject
Pong   a bad smell
Poofter   a homosexual man
Port   a suitcase
Postie   a mail delivery person
Pot   a ten ounce beer glass (Queensland and Victoria only)
Pozzy/Pozzie/Possie   position
Prang   a car crash, accident
Prawn   shrimp
Preggers   pregnant
Pre-loved   second-hand, used
Prezzie   a gift, present
Pubes   pubic hair
Pull your head in   mind your own business
Puffed   out of breath, tired
Pug   a boxer
Puka   large extended stomach
Puke   vomit

Aussie's love a **barbie** and a prawn on the barbie is "**the duck's guts**".

Punch-up   a fight
Punter   a gambler; bets money on horse or dog races
Pushing up daisies   to be dead
Put down   to kill an animal
Put the hard word on   ask a favour, loan
Put the mockers on   to cause bad luck
Quack   1. a bad doctor; 2. unqualified
Quake Isles   New Zealand
Quart-pot   a billycan
Queen   a homosexual
Queer   a homosexual
Queer bird   strange person, odd
Quick as greased lightning   very quick
Quick march   hurry up
Quick quid   easy money
Quick snort   a hasty alcoholic drink
Quickie   a short sexual encounter
Quid, make a   earn a living
Quid, not the full   person with a low IQ
Quim   female genitalia
Quits   gives up easily
Quitter   to give up easily
Quoit   bum, anus
R & R   rest and recreation
RS   rat shit; feeling bad
RSL   Returned Services League
Rabbit food   green vegetables, lettuce etc.
Rabbit on   talk nonsense
Rack off   please leave
Rack up   amass

A **punch-up** followed the **barney** between Big Bruce and **queer bird Nigel**.

Radical   great, fantastic

Rafferty's rules   no rules at all

Rag   1. newspaper; 2. argue; 3. gossip; 4. handkerchief

Rage   party

Rage on   continue to party

Rager   a person who parties hard

Rain dance   a ceremony believed to cause rain

Raining cats and dogs   very heavy rain

Rank and file   general people

Rapt   overjoyed

Rare as rocking horse shit   uncommon

Rare as hen's teeth   vary rare

Rat shit   no good, bad, lousy

Ratbag   an unreliable person, fool

Ration bag   a calico bag used to carry food

Rattle the dags   get a move on, hurry up

Rattler   a railway train

Ratty   1. worn out; 2. mildly eccentric

Rave   1. big dance party; 2. type of dance music; 3. animated conversation

Raw prawn   behaved offensively

Ready to drop   very pregnant

Reckon   1. absolutely; 2. suppose

Red centre   the centre of Australia

Red Ned   cheap red wine

Red steer   a bushfire

Redback   1. a $20 note; 2. a small poisonous spider with a red back

Reefer   a marijuana cigarette

Ref   referee

Refadex   Queensland street directory

Reffo   refugee

Bert used to be **flat broke** until one day he discovered how to invest by reading the financial **rag**.

Rego   motor vehicle registration

Reject   socially unacceptable person

Rellies   relatives, relations, kin

Rep   representative

Retard   clumsy or awkward person

Rev   engine revolution

Richard Cranium   a dickhead

Ridgy-didge   1. truth, on the level; 2. original, genuine; 3. refrigerator

Right, that'd be   accepting bad news

Righty-o/Righto   yes, okay

Ringbark   to kill a tree by cutting the bark off around the trunk

Ringdinger   a two-stroke motorcycle

Ringer   1. fast sheep shearer; 2. person or thing that resembles another

Ring-in   substitute, deceive

Rip   a dangerous under-current at the beach

Rip into   begin rapidly, eagerly

Rip off   1. a poor deal, overpriced item; 2. knockoff

Rip snorter   fantastic, outstanding

Ripe   1. something gone off; 2. eager, keen; 3. drunk; 4. obscene

Ripper   great, good

Ripper, you little   exclamation of delight to good news

Rissole   1. round meat or fish patty; 2. nickname for an RSL club

Road train   a rig of two, three or four trucks drawn by a prime mover

Roadie   1. last drink; 2. drink you take when leaving a function

Rock along   travel to, go, visit

Rock on   1. come on; 2. continue

Rock up   to arrive or turn up

Rogues' gallery   police file collection of criminals' photographs

Roll a joint   roll a marijuana cigarette

Rollie   a cigarette that you roll

Rolling in it very wealthy
Roo a kangaroo
Roo bar a bar fixed to a vehicle to protect it against hitting kangaroos
Root for cheer for, encourage
Root rat one who is always looking for sex
Rooted 1. totally exhausted; 2. broken beyond repair; 3. abuse; go away!
Ropeable very angry
Rort a fraud
Rotten drunk
Rouse lose one's temper, chastise
Rub it in remind one of their mistakes and failures
Rubbish 1. criticise; 2. garbage, trash; 3. tease
Ruckus a commotion
Rugrat ankle biter, small child
Rug up dress warmly
Run on the smell of an oily rag a car running on very little fuel
Runabout a small motor boat
Runs diarrhoea
Runt 1. a small person; 2. smallest in the litter
Rush 1. strong feeling of exhilaration and pleasure; 2. very busy
Saltie a salt water crocodile
Salvo a member of the Salvation Army
Sammie a sandwich
Sandgroper a person from Western Australia
Sandshoe jogger, sneaker, trainer
Sanga/Sanger sandwich
Sav a saveloy; a type of sausage
Savvy 1. understand; 2. know; 3. intelligence; 4. commonsense
Scab 1. strike breaker; 2. stingy person; 3. bludge from someone
Scallywag mischievious person, rascal

Good
old fashioned
toasted cheese **sanga**.

Scalper   one who buys function tickets and then sells them at a higher price
Scaly   a crocodile
Schooner   15 ounce glass of beer (Australia wide except South Australia)
Scone   1. the head; 2. a light cake or biscuit
Scoob   a marijuana cigarette, reefer
Scorcher   a very hot day
Scrag   unattractive woman
Scratchie   instant lottery ticket
Screamer   one who gets drunk on very little alcohol
Scrounge   to borrow or collect something
Scrub   bushland
Scrub up well   1. to be well dressed; 2. look good
Scrubbers   1. wild cattle; 2. unattractive woman
See ya   goodbye, see you later
Seedy   feeling sick; especially after a drinking spree
Semi   a large truck
Send her down Huey   send down the rain
Servo   a service station
Shack   a simple house
Shades   sunglasses
Shag on a rock, stands out like a   very obvious
Shaggy dog story   a very long story or joke with a pointless ending
Shanghai   1. sling-shot; 2. involve one in an activity against their wishes
Shanty   a small bush hotel
Shark bait   a swimmer in shark infested waters
Shark biscuit   one who is new to surfing
She'll be right   everything will be okay
Sheila   a young woman
Shindig   a lively party
Shit house   1. poor quality; 2. toilet

Shonky poor quality goods
Shoot through leave unexpectedly
Shout buy a round of drinks
Shove off go away, scat
Show pony one who is concerned with appearances
Sick 1. totally excellent, cool; 2. disgusting, revolting
Sickie take a day off sick from work
Sicko disgusting revolting person, depraved
Silly duffer a silly person
Silvertail upper crust, social climber
Singlet tank top, vest
Siphon the python to urinate
Skeeter a mosquito
Skidmark mark of faeces on underwear
Skids brakes
Skin and blister sister
Skin flint miser
Skinny dipping nude swimming
Skite to boast or brag
Skol drink alcohol in one gulp
Sky pilot a clergyman, priest
Sky rocket pocket
Slab a 24 pack of beer
Slab hut a bush dwelling constructed from timber slabs
Slammer prison
Slash to urinate
Sleepout a porch or verandah converted to a bedroom
Slice of the cake a share in the profits
Sling 1. a bribe; 2. tip
Slog hard work

Bob did time in the **slammer** for **knocking off** a **one tonner** and driving it through the front window of the **milk bar**.

Sloshed   very intoxicated

Slouch hat   Australian Army hat

Sly grog   alcohol sold by an unlicensed vendor

Smoko   smoke, tea or coffee break

Snags   sausages

Snake's hiss   to urinate, piss

Snakey   bad-tempered, irritable

Snooze   sleep, doze, nap

Snorker   a sausage

Snow/Snowy   a person with white or blonde hair

Snug as a bug in a rug   cosy

So long   goodbye

Sook   a weak timid person, a cry baby

Southpaw   left-handed person

Sozzled   intoxicated

Sparky   an electrician

Sparrow fart   dawn

Aussie's love to throw a few **snags** on the **barbie.**

Spat   minor argument, fight

Specs   glasses, spectacles

Spell   to have a rest

Spew   1. to vomit; 2. very angry; 3. disappointed at something

Spewin'   very angry, upset

Spiffy   excellent, great

Spin out   1. greatly amazed; 2. a vehicle skids and spins off the road

Spit the dummy   upset

Spruiker   a person who forcefully addresses prospective customers

Sprung   caught doing wrong

Spud   a potato

Spunky   attractive sexy person

Squib   a coward

Squirt   1. insignificant; 2. short person; 3. little child; 4. male urination
Squizz   to look
Starkers   1. totally naked; 2. insane
Station   homestead, ranch
Stayer   an animal (horse) or person of great endurance
Stick-up   a robbery at gun point
Stickybeak   a nosey person
Stirrer   one who causes trouble
Stock route   a track or road used by a drover
Stockman   a person who looks after livestock on a large farming property
Stoked   to be very happy
Stone-broke   no money
Stoned   drunk, intoxicated or under the influence of drugs
Stonkered   1. defeated; 2. drunk; 3. exhausted; 4. incapacitated
Storm stick   umbrella
Stoush   a brawl or fight
Straddie   North and South Stradbroke Island; near Brisbane, Queensland
Strapped for cash   short of money
Strewth   1. exclamation of surprise; 2. exclamation of irritation
Strides   trousers or pants
Strine   Australian slang
Stroppy   in a bad temper
Stubbies   men's work shorts
Stubby   a small bottle of beer
Stubby cooler   insulation casing for a stubby
Stuck-up   haughty, conceited
Stud   a male who considers himself extremely sexually attractive
Stuff   1. personal belongings; 2. render useless, ruin
Stuff it!   exclamation of frustration or anger
Stuffed   1. tired; 2. worn out; 3. broken; 4. full of food

Stuffed, I'll be   expression of surprise

Stunned mullet   dazed

Stunner   thing or person of striking beauty

Subbie   a sub-contractor

Suck face   French kiss

Sunbake   sunbathe

Sunnies   sunglasses

Sunshine State   Queensland

Super   1. personal retirement fund; 2. leaded petrol; 3. very good, great

Surfie   person devoted to surfing, surfboard riding

Swag   a roll of blankets

Swagman/Swaggie   a tramp

Swansong   a last performance

Sweet tooth   liking sweet foods, lollies etc

Swipe   steal

Sydneysider   a person who lives in Sydney

TB   tuberculosis

TLC   tender loving care

Ta   Thank you

Tacho   tachometer

Tad   little bit

Taddie   tadpole

Tag   to follow closely

Tag along   join in with others

Tail   1. buttocks; 2. follow close behind

Tail throwing   pulling a beast down by the tail

Tailgate   drive very close to the vehicle in front

Take a gander   have a look

Take a sickie   take a work sick day when you're not sick

Take a squizz   have a look

The number one thing on a **surfie's** mind is catching a **bonzer** wave.

Take-away   take-out food

Take some pickies/piccies   take photographs

Tall poppie   an important, successful person

Tall poppie syndrome   to criticise important, successful people

Tallie   750ml bottle of beer

Tally   counting

Tangle foot   one who's clumsy on his feet

Tanked   intoxicated, drunk

Tarp   a tarpaulin

Tart   an immoral woman, prostitute

Tassie   Tasmania

Taswegian   a person from Tasmania

Tat   a tattoo

Tea   evening meal

Ben **tucked** into his **take-away** the minute he arrived home.

Tear into   attack physically or verbally

Tear strips off   admonish severely

Tear-arse   a wild reckless person, fast driver

Tear-jerker   something very sad

Tech   Technical college

Techie   technician

Technicolour yawn   to vomit

Tee up   to organise a meeting

Tellie   television

Territorian   a person from the Northern Territory

The axe   to be dismissed, sacked

The big A   axed; get the sack, dismissed

The big C   cancer

The big spit   to vomit

The box   television

The Cross   Kings Cross, Sydney

The Don Sir Donald Bradman; the best ever batsman
The finger offensive gesture made by holding up the middle finger
The missus wife
The Rock Uluru, Ayers Rock
The sticks 1. in the country; 2. goal posts in a game of rugby or AFL
The Territory The Northern Territory
Thick dopey, fool
Thick-skinned one who does not like criticism or verbal abuse
Thin on top going bald
Thingo could be anything
This arvo this afternoon
Thongs cheap rubber backless sandals, flip-flops
Throw down a small bottle of beer that can be drunk quickly
Thunder box a toilet, dunny
Tick 1. credit; 2. moment or instant; 3. check mark
Ticker the heart
Tickets on yourself to have a high opinion of yourself
Tickle the ivories play the piano
Tickle the Peter to steal minor amounts from a till or cash register
Tiddly slightly drunk, tipsy
Tide's out beer glass needs topping up
Tie the knot to wed
Tiff an argument or a spat
Tiger country rough bushland
Tight 1. unwilling to spend; 2. close; nearly even
Tight as a fish's arse a very miserly person
Tim Tam chocolate sandwich biscuit coated in chocolate
Tin arsed a very lucky person
Tinned dog canned meat, camp pie
Tinnie 1. a can of beer; 2. a small aluminium boat; 3. lucky

Tip   1. offer a racing tip to someone; 2. rubbish dump

Tipsy   slightly drunk

Tit   female breast

Tit for tat   a hat

Toey   1. nervous, apprehensive; 2. keen, ready to go

Togs   a bathing suit, clothes

Tomahawk   a small axe

Too right   definitely

Top drop   a good bottle of wine or a good beer

Top end   northern part of the Northern Territory

Tosser   annoying person, jerk

Trackie daks   tracksuit pants

Trackies   track suit

Troppo   gone mad, insane

Trots   1. having diarrhoea; 2. harness horse racing

Truckie   a truck driver

True blue   1. genuine; 2. a loyal person

Tuck in   to eat, have a meal

Tucker   food

Tucker bag   a food carrying bag

Turps   1. alcoholic drink; 2. turpentine

Turps, hit the   a drinking binge

The **trots** is a horse race focusing on the horse's gait and requires the horse to pull a two-wheeled cart called a sulky.

Tweeds   trousers, pants

Twinkle toes   a good dancer

Twit   a dull, stupid person

Two-pot screamer   a very cheap drunk

Two-up   a gambling game with two coins, heads or tails

Tyke   a Roman Catholic

U-ee   a U turn on the road

Ugg boots/Uggies   boots made of sheepskin

Ugly as sin   a very ugly person
Umpie   umpire
Umpteen   many, large amount
Unco   awkward, clumsy person
Under the weather   1. feeling poorly; 2. hungover
Underdaks   underpants
Underdog   a team or organisation not expected to win
Undies   underpants
Uni   university
Unit   a flat or apartment
Unreal!   excellent!
Unsung hero   a person who is not celebrated or recognised
Unwind   to relax, take it easy
Up a gum tree   in difficulties
Up and about   active after an illness or sleep
Up at sparrow fart   rising very early
Up oneself   have a high opinion of oneself
Up somebody, to get   to berate somebody
Up the creek in a barbed wire canoe without a paddle   bad situation
Up the duff   pregnant
Up to putty   no good, worthless
Urger   a racecourse tipster
Useful as tits on a bull   1. incompetent person; 2. useless person or thing
User   1. one who exploits other people; 2. drug addict
Ute   a utility; open-backed work vehicle
VB   Victoria bitter, a popular Australian beer
Vacuum   a vacuum cleaner
Valley, the   Fortitude Valley, Brisbane
Vamoose   depart quickly
Vee-dub   a Volkswagen car

Veg out   relax

Vegemite   a dark-brown savoury sandwich spread made from yeast extract

Veggies   vegetables

Vego   a vegetarian

Verbal diarrhoea   constant talking

Vet   1. Veterinary surgeon; 2. a war veteran

Vibe   1. atmosphere; 2. feeling; 3. rhythm; 4. signals sent out to someone

Vinnie's   St Vincent de Paul charity shop

Vino   wine

Vocal   vocabulary

WACA   1. Western Australian Cricket Association; 2. Perth cricket ground

Wacked   1. exhausted; 2. out of it

Waddie   a baton or club

Wadjamacallit   something you don't know the name of

Waffle   talking nonsense

Wag   1. an amusing person, a joker; 2. skip school, truancy

Walkabout   1. gone missing; 2. an extended trip or tour on foot

Wallop   thrash, punch with force

Walloper   a policeman

Wally   1. a stupid person; 2. wallet

Waltzing Matilda   1. carry one's swag; 2. well known Australian song

Wanker   1. a stupid person; 2. an arrogant person; 3. an amusing person

Wanna   want to

Wanna-be   one who tries very hard without success

Washer   a face towel

Wasted   1. exhausted; 2. under the effects of alcohol or drugs

Water bag   a portable water container

Water the horse   to urinate

Watering hole   one's favourite pub or hotel

Way   extremely

Weaner   a calf no longer feeding from its mother
Wedding tackle   a male's sexual organs
Wedgie   prank where one's pants are grabbed and pulled up sharply
Wee   urine, to urinate
Weekend warrior   person in the army reserve
Weekender   holiday house
Weenies   small frankfurts
Well-heeled   a wealthy person
Well-to-do   rich, prosperous
Wellies   Wellington boots or gumboots
Wet, the   rainy season in Northern Australia from December to March
Wettie   a wetsuit
Whacked   drunk, intoxicated
Whaler   a bush nomad
Wharfie   a dock worker
What's the damage?   how much does it cost?
Whatsaname   used when unable to recall real name of person or thing
When the eagle shits   pay day
Whew   expressing relief
Whiffie   offensive smell
Whinge   to whimper, complain
Whip around   collect money
Whipped   defeated
White pointers   topless female sunbathers or bathers
Whirlybird   a helicopter
White ant   to go behind someone's back
White leghorn   a female lawn bowler
Whoop whoop   a long way away
Whose shout?   whose turn to buy the drinks?
Wifey   your wife or spouse

Wig warmer   a hat
Willie   a penis
Willy willy   a brief dust storm of cyclonic nature
Wimp   a weak person
Windies   West Indian cricket team
Wing-ding   a big party
Wino   alcoholic, addicted to wine
Winkers   the eyes
Witchety grub   a large white grub found in wood
Wizz   to urinate
Wobbly   losing your temper
Wog   1. flu or a cold; 2. annoying insect; 3. person of Mediterranean origin
Wombat   one who eats, roots and leaves
Wonky   1. unstable, unsteady; 2. poor condition
Wooden spoon   a prize for coming last
Woofer   a dog
Woofter   a homosexual man
Woolshed   a shed where sheep are shorn
Woop woop   1. middle of nowhere; 2. small insignificant town
Wouldn't be dead for quids   to be alive and well
Wouldn't piss on you if you were on fire   expression of utter contempt
Wouldn't work in an iron lung   a very lazy person
Wowser   1. a non drinker; 2. a puritan
Wrung-out   exhausted, tired-out
Wuss   timid person, coward
XXXX   Queensland Four X Beer
Ya   you, your
Yabber   talk a lot, chat
Yabbie/Yabby   Australian freshwater crayfish
Yack   1. talk a lot; 2. chat; 3. vomit

The freshwater **yabby** is often caught for food.

Yachtie   a person who sails on yachts

Yacker/Yakka/Yakker   hard work

Yahoo   1. a reckless person, lout, uncouth; 2. exclamation of delight

Yair/Yeah   yes

Yank   1. an American; 2. to tell a lie

Yank tank   large American manufactured car

Yap   talk continuously

Yarn   1. a story; 2. talking with somebody

Yikes   mild exclamation of concern

Yobbo   a rude person, lout, hooligan

Yodel   to vomit

Yonks   a long period of time

You beaut/beauty   something good

You wish   an expression referring to one with unrealistic expectations

Young'un   a youngster

You're not wrong   you are right

Youse   plural for you

Yowie   mythical monster

Yuck   expression of disgust, unpleasant

Yuppie   young urban professional person with a high disposable income

Z grade   the lowest quality

Zac/Zack   old currency (sixpence) now five cents

Zap   1. cook in the microwave; 2. annihilate; 3. electric shock; 4. exhausted

Zebra crossing   a pedestrian crossing with broad white painted lines

Zeds   sleep, snooze

Ziff   unshaven, beard

Zilch   nil, nothing

Zip   zero, nothing

Zit   acne, pimples

Zonked   1. very tired; 2. drunk

Notes